Learn Japanese In 7 DAYS!

The Ultimate Crash Course to Learning the Basics of the Japanese Language in No Time

By Dagny Taggart

© **Copyright 2014**

All rights reserved. No portion of this book may be reproduced -mechanically, electronically, or by any other means, including photocopying- without the permission of the publisher.

Disclaimer

The information provided in this book is designed to provide helpful information on the subjects discussed. The author's books are only meant to provide the reader with the basics knowledge of a certain language, without any warranties regarding whether the student will, or will not, be able to incorporate and apply all the information provided. Although the writer will make her best effort share her insights, language learning is a difficult task, and each person needs a different timeframe to fully incorporate a new language. This book, nor any of the author's books constitute a promise that the reader will learn a certain language within a certain timeframe.

Table of Contents

Introduction: Are You Ready For An Amazing Journey?
   How to Use This Book

Chapter 1: Getting The Pronunciation Down

Chapter 2: Hiragana and Katakana
   Hiragana
   Practice Questions
   Katakana
   Practice Questions

Chapter 3: Basic Greetings (*Hi, Good Morning, Thanks*)
   Key Greetings Review
   Practice Questions

Chapter 4: It's Time To Introduce Yourself!

Chapter 5: Asking Questions (Where Would We Be Without Them?)
   Key Vocabulary
   Example Sentences
   Answering A Question
   Practice Questions

Chapter 6: Numbers!
   How Old Are You?
   What Time Is It?
   Practice Questions

Chapter 7: "*What Are You Doing?*" An Introduction to Verbs
   Ru-verbs
   Practice Questions
   U-Verbs
   Negative Form
   Practice Questions

Chapter 8: Hey, Let's Go Shopping!
   What Do You Want?
   Example Dialogue

Chapter 9: Are *You* Hungry? Looking for a Restaurant...
   Getting There (Or Anywhere)
   Sample Dialogue

    Present Progressive Verbs
    Multiple Verbs
    Past Tense Verbs
    Practice Questions
    Making An Order
    Practice Questions

Chapter 10: Riding the Train (You Won't Get Lost, I Promise!)
    Example Dialogue
    Where Do You Want to Go?
    Practice Questions

Conclusion: Now Embark on Your Own Adventure!

Preview Of "Learn Spanish In 7 DAYS! - The Ultimate Crash Course To Learn The Basics of the Spanish Language In No Time"

Dedicated to those who love going beyond their own frontiers.

Keep on traveling,

Dagny Taggart

Introduction
Are You Ready For An Amazing Journey?

Japan has a long history of being isolated from the rest of the world, seemingly inaccessible to the West, and to some the perception still lingers of a mysterious land with a strange, totally foreign culture and a language so difficult that Jesuit missionaries in the 16th century referred to it as "the devil's tongue." Many Japanese themselves carry the assumption that foreigners cannot understand their culture or language, and are sometimes shocked to hear a non-Japanese speak Japanese fluently. And indeed, such feelings would not seem unreasonable. A writing system composed of two alphabets and thousands of complex characters, grammar that tends to order sentences in the exact opposite of English, and a lack of common roots that help make learning languages like Spanish or German easy all seem daunting to the beginner. However, by reading this book, you're taking your first step to reversing that perception. Learning Japanese is something anyone can do, and like any great journey, you just need to start with the first step. In fact, Japanese as a spoken language has many easy aspects- consistent pronunciation familiar to English speakers, flexible grammar, and a host of English loan words among them.

Until the past several decades, very few foreigners attempted to learn the language, and the treasures of Japanese culture were for the most part kept within Japan's borders, but worldwide Japanese study has since seen an exponential boom, and for good reason. A major economic power, Japanese companies and products have a worldwide influence, and many study the language for business. Others are drawn to the rich traditional culture of Japan, influenced by a unique history that spawned the samurai, ninja, tea ceremony, and Zen Buddhism that have become part of the world's imagination. Still others come to the language through Japanese pop culture such as anime, manga, J-pop and video games. Whatever your motivation, your journey starts with a single step. Let this book open the gate for you to start your journey to learning Japanese!

How to Use This Book

There's never been a better time to learn a language than now. In the past, contact with a foreign language, especially one like Japanese, may have been hard to come by, and learners were often isolated alone with their textbooks. However, we now live in a much more globalized world, and the internet has opened virtually limitless information to anyone with a connection. There's a whole world of Japanese waiting for you, and think of this book as a guide to the first stage of your journey. A lifetime's worth of Japanese media is available for free online, so try watching or listening to some, and look for the expressions you've learned. Even if you can't understand everything, you'll be pleasantly surprised to notice what you'll learn in this book, starting from the very first chapter, pop up frequently. You may worry about the speed at which native Japanese is spoken, but, helpfully, many Japanese television shows feature on-screen subtitles. Even with a very small vocabulary, listening will help you get a feel for how Japanese sounds, and without even realizing it you'll start mimicking these sounds yourself. The base of knowledge you gain here will be the seed that takes root when you step into the world of native Japanese. Without hesitating, dive in and start immersing yourself in this material as much as you can. Not only will the language basics taught here start to take flight, you'll learn a lot about a new culture and, if you can find media you like, have a lot of fun too.

This book is generally organized so that practical concerns of getting by in Japanese are accompanied both by the introduction of new gramumar points, lists of vocabulary, and plenty of examples and practice questions. The most essential phrases will be introduced along with explanations, and the vocabulary is chosen to help expand what you can say, giving you variations with which to express yourself. Keep a notebook handy while reading so you can write down new words and phrases that pop up. Making flashcards, whether manually or using a computer program, is an efficient and fun way to remember new words. Once you've remembered the vocab, try using them together with the grammatical points introduced to make your own sentences!

Chapter 1: Getting The Pronunciation Down

Compared to languages like Chinese or French, Japanese is an easy language to pronounce if you can comprehend a few basic principles. First of all, unlike English, you can always know how to pronounce a word based on its spelling, as the Japanese "alphabet" is composed of always-consistent sounds instead of the shifting, ever-changing pronunciation of English letters. For example, think of the English word *read*. Based on the context , it can be pronounced in two different ways. This is never the case in Japanese. Second, vowels are always given their long reading. *A* as in *car* or *father,* never as in *apple* or *ace. I* is pronounced like *ee* in *meet, u* like the *oo* in *root. E* is read like in *met,* and *o* like in *no* or *snow.* Generally, there are no exceptions to this rule, which means the Japanese language is composed of far fewer sounds than English (about a hundred in Japanese, as opposed to over 10,000 in English).

Here are some examples of Japanese words, along with their pronunciation:

watashi (I, me, myself) = wah – tah – shee
tomodachi (friend) = toe – moe – dah – chee
Nihon (Japan) = Nee – hoe – n
eki (station) = eh – kee
umi (ocean) = oo – mee

Thinking of Japanese words you may already know such as *sushi*, *origami*, *tsunami, tofu,* and *ramen* can help you realize the basics of Japanese pronunciation. However, be wary of words you may be mispronouncing. Some common culprits include *sake* (sah – keh, not sah – kee) and *karaoke* (kah – rah – oh – keh, not kah – ree – oh – key).

One exception is the *su* syllable, which is sometimes (but not always) shortened to sound like *-s.* For example, the word *suki* (like) is almost always pronounced like *skee* rather than *soo-kee*, and names like Daisuke and Yusuke *Dai-skey* and *Yoo-skey* rather than *Dai-soo-kee* or *Yoo-soo-kee*. As you start speaking more Japanese you'll naturally know when a word is read like this, but in this book it will always be noted to help you get used to it.

There are two other features of Japanese pronunciation you should know about. One is the way vowels are elongated. Sometimes a vowel will appear twice in a Japanese word. Unlike in English, where the pronunciation changes (think of *rot* vs. *root*), in Japanese the same sound is elongated. For example, in the word *ookii* (big) the *oh* and *ee* sounds are voiced twice, in effect elongating the vowels. Also, when a *u* appears after an *o,* the effect is the same: voicing the *o* sound twice rather than reading *oh – oo.* For example, *arigatou* (thank you) is read *ah-ree-gah-toh* with an elongated final *oh* instead of *a-ree-*

gah-toh-oo. The same goes for an *i* after an *e,* so *suiei* (swimming) is read with an elongated *eh* sound rather than *eh-ee*. In the next section, we'll try reading using the Japanese alphabet(s), and some of these rules will become more clear.

The other feature is consonant doubling. When writing Japanese with English letters, this is expressed by writing two consonants. Some common examples include *gakkou* (school), *kippu* (ticket), and *kissaten* (cafe). In this case, there is a short pause before the consonant is pronounced, with the first letter representing this pause. More precisely, your tongue will touch the roof of your mouth as the consonant is pronounced. It may help to think of *gakkou* as being read like *gak-koh* instead of *gah-koh*. Of course, nothing beats simply hearing the proper pronunciation and imitating it yourself, something within reach of anyone with an internet connection. This feature of pronunciation too has a way of being expressed in Japanese lettering that we'll look at in the next section.

Keeping these rules in mind, try pronouncing this list of some of the most common Japanese nouns:

asagohan (breakfast)
bangohan (dinner)
eiga (movie)
eigo (English)
gohan (rice)
hana (flower)
hirugohan (lunch)
hito (person)
ie (house)
inu (dog)
kao (face)
kodomo (child)
kokoro (heart, mind)
michi (road)
mizu (water)
neko (cat)
nihongo (Japanese)
niku (meat)
okaasan (mother)
okane (money)
onna (woman)
otoko (man)
otousan (father)
pan (bread)
sakana (fish)

tamago (egg)
te (hand)
toki (time)
tori (bird)
yasai (vegetable)

Chapter 2: Hiragana and Katakana

Hiragana

As you're probably aware, Japanese uses a writing system completely different from that of English. What you may not have known is that virtually all Japanese people can also read and write English letters (often more beautifully than native English speakers!) and all elementary school students learn how to write Japanese with English letters. This is called *romaji,* and makes up one of the four writing systems used in Japanese, the others being *hiragana, katakana,* and *kanji.* The first two are different styles of the Japanese phonetic alphabet, which differs from the English alphabet in that it is composed of consistently pronounced sounds rather than letters. The former, *hiragana,* is generally used for Japanese words, while *katakana* is used to write Japanese transliterations of foreign loan words. To use food as an example, *sushi, tempura,* and *soba* would be written in *hiragana,* while *hanbaagaa* (hamburger), *pankeeki* (pancake), and *furaido poteto* (fried potato, AKA french fries) would be written in *katakana.* *Kanji* are pictogram-like characters borrowed from Chinese that express meaning rather than sound.

Let's take the word for the Japanese language itself as an example of the ways a word can be written. In *romaji,* it is written as *nihongo,* in *hiragana* as にほんご (に=ni ほ=ho ん=n ご=go). Both of these ways of writing indicate how the word is read. In *kanji,* however, the word is written 日本語. In this case, each character represents a piece of meaning rather than a sound. 日(ni), one of the most basic and frequently appearing *kanji,* means *sun,* and is also used to mean *day.* 本(hon) can express a variety of meanings, but here means *source.* Together, these make up *Nihon,* the word for Japan, which, as you've probably already guessed, literally means "the source of the sun," an idea from ancient Japanese mythology (as well as the source of Japan's nickname "Land of the Rising Sun.") Lastly, 語(go) means *language.* Put them together, and you have *nihongo,* the Japanese language. With over 3000 such characters used in daily Japanese, and many, many more in specialized texts, mastering *kanji* can take many years (most Japanese don't learn all the *kanji* necessary to read a newspaper until high school), but this is no reason to give up on learning Japanese. Even learning just the *hiragana* and *katakana* alphabets will hugely improve how much you can get by in Japan, and most signs and basic materials written in *kanji* feature readings in *hiragana.* Even *manga,* Japanese comic books, often have the readings in *hiragana* written above the *kanji.*

Learning *hiragana* and *katakana* will also help your Japanese pronunciation. Even *romaji* can be misleading for an English speaker, and using the Japanese phonetic alphabet eliminates any ambiguity as to how to read a word. Taking the time to remember these characters will give you a nice boost in the beginning stage of your Japanese study. Try breaking them up and studying them in pieces. Usually one week to memorize the *hiragana* and one for *katakana* should be enough even with only a little bit of practice a day, and of course you can memorize them faster if you put in more time. As with vocabulary, flashcards are a great tool. Subsequent chapters of this book will offer examples and problem sets written in Japanese, so even if you haven't memorized all the characters fully yet, consider the challenge of trying to remember and read them as part of your practice! Don't think you have to have all the *hiragana* and *katakana* completely memorized before moving on to the next section: learn as you go, referring back to the chart or your flashcards when you need to.

So, without further ado, let's take a look at the basic list of *hiragana*.

	あ a	い i	う u	え e	お o
k	か ka	き ki	く ku	け ke	こ ko
s	さ sa	し shi	す su	せ se	そ so
t	た ta	ち chi	つ tsu	て te	と to
n	な na	に ni	ぬ nu	ね ne	の no
h	は ha	ひ hi	ふ fu	へ he	ほ ho
m	ま ma	み mi	む mu	め me	も mo
y	や ya		ゆ yu		よ yo
r	ら ra	り ri	る ru	れ re	ろ ro
w	わ wa				を wo
	ん n					

You'll notice that Japanese pronunciation differs from English in some ways. For example, in place of a character for *si* there is *shi*, *tsu* for *tu*, and *fu* for *hu*. This is due to the limited number of sounds in Japanese. Though you'll quickly get used to these differences as you learn more words, they should be noted carefully in the beginning stage. Also worthy of note is the character ん, unique in that it is the only syllable that doesn't end in a vowel. Thus, there are times when you can only tell a word's pronunciation by seeing it in *hiragana* rather than *romaji*. One example is *kinen*. Looking at the *romaji*, the word could be written as either きねん or きんえん. However, these two have differing pronunciation, and in fact completely different meanings. きねん is read as it appears in English letters *(kee-ne-n)*, and means *memorial*. きんえん is read with a short pause after the *n* sound *(kee-n-en)*, and means *no smoking*. Think of the ん as a separate sound from the vowel that follows it, rather than connecting them as you would in English. Other examples of this tricky difference in pronunciation include かに *(kah-nee)* and かんい *(kah-n-ee)*, meaning *crab* and *simplicity,* respectively, which you'll want to remember when ordering at a restaurant!

In the last section, the pronunciation of double consonants such as *gakkou* (school) and *kippu* (ticket) was briefly introduced. In Japanese, this is expressed with a small つ(tsu) before the doubled consonant. Thus, the above two words are written as がっこう and きっぷ, respectively. Though reading these words like *gatsukou* or *kitsupu* will surely amuse any Japanese friends you make, avoid this confusing this marker with a regular つ.

There are a few variations on this basic list of sounds. A " mark added to a hiragana means the consonant is voiced: expressed in *romaji,*, *k* becomes *g*, *h* becomes *b*, *s* becomes *z*, and *t* becomes *d*. A small circle makes an *h* sound into a *p*. Another way *hiragana* can be expanded is by adding a small や(ya), ゆ (yu), or よ(yo) to a sound ending in i. For example, り(ri) can become りゅ (ryu), し(shi) can become しゃ(sha), き(ki) can become きょ(kyo), and so on.

Considering these variations, the list of *hiragana* can be expanded as follows.

	ya	yu	yo
K	きゃ kya	きゅ kyu	きょ kyo
S	しゃ sha	しゅ shu	しょ sho
T	ちゃ cha	ちゅ chu	ちょ cho
N	にゃ	にゅ	にょ

	nyo	nyu	nyo
H	ひゃ hya	ひゅ hyu	ひょ hyo
M	みゃ mya	みゅ myu	みょ myo
r	りゃ rya	りゅ ryu	りょ ryo

	a	i	u	e	o	ya	yu	yo
g	が ga	ぎ gi	ぐ gu	げ ge	ご go	ぎゃ gya	ぎゅ gyu	ぎょ gyo
z	ざ za	じ ji	ず zu	ぜ ze	ぞ zo	じゃ ja	じゅ ju	じょ jo
d	だ da	ぢ* ji	づ dzu	で de	ど do			
b	ば ba	び bi	ぶ bu	べ be	ぼ bo	びゃ bya	びゅ byu	びょ byo
p	ぱ pa	ぴ pi	ぷ pu	ぺ pe	ぽ po	ぴゃ pya	ぴゅ pyu	ぴょ pyo

As this character has the same pronunciation as the more common じ, it is rarely used.

Practice Questions

Once you've looked over the hiragana a few times and maybe practiced with your flashcards, give this matching list of Japanese words you may already know a try. Even if you can't read every letter in a word, try your best to match based on the ones you recognize. After checking your answers, challenge it again on the next day. You might be surprised by the progress you make! (answers on next page)

1. えだまめ
2. おりがみ
3. かぶき
4. からて
5. きもの
6. さけ

a. kimono
b. sumo
c. hibachi
d. origami
e. futon
f. sudoku

7. さようなら　　　　　　　　　　　g. teriyaki
8. しいたけ　　　　　　　　　　　　h. haiku
9. すうどく　　　　　　　　　　　　i. tofu
10. すきやき　　　　　　　　　　　j. edamame
11. すし　　　　　　　　　　　　　k. sake
12. すもう　　　　　　　　　　　　l. tempura
13. つなみ　　　　　　　　　　　　m. sushi
14. てりやき　　　　　　　　　　　n. kabuki
15. てんぷら　　　　　　　　　　　o. sukiyaki
16. とうふ　　　　　　　　　　　　p. karate
17. はいく　　　　　　　　　　　　q. miso
18. ひばち　　　　　　　　　　　　r. sayonara
19. ふとん　　　　　　　　　　　　s. manga
20. まんが　　　　　　　　　　　　t. shitake
21. みそ　　　　　　　　　　　　　u. tsunami

Answer Key

1. j 2. d 3. n 4. p 5. a 6. k 7. r   8. t 9. f 10. o 11. m 12. b 13. u 14. g 15. l 16. i 17. h 18. c 19. e 20. s 21. q

You've probably noticed how reading a character in Japanese rather than the English alphabet will improve your pronunciation.   For example, すもう (sumo) and さようなら (sayonara) both feature an elongated *o* sound (indicated by a う following a sound ending in *o*) that is more obvious when viewed in Japanese rather than English.

For your next challenge, let's practice remembering *hiragana* while also reviewing some of the common words introduced in the last chapter.   By looking at the *hiragana* together with the English meaning, see if you can reproduce the word in *romaji*.

1. とき (time) --15. ばんごはん (dinner)
2. えいご (English) --------------------------------16. やさい (vegetable)
3. おとこ　(man) ----------------------------------17. はな (flower)
4. こども (child) ----------------------------------18. ごはん(rice)
5. こころ (heart, mind) ---------------------------19. にく (meat)
6. いぬ (dog) --------------------------------------20. とり (bird)
7. かお (face) -------------------------------------21. おかあさん (mother)
8. て (hand) ----------------------------------- 22. みず (water)

9. おんな (woman) ---------------------------------23. おかね (money)
10. ねこ   (cat)   --24.   あさごはん (breakfast)
11. おとうさん (father) -----------------------------25. ひるごはん (lunch)
12. みち (road) --26. いえ (house)
13. ひと (person) ---------------------------------------27. にほんご (Japanese)
14. たまご (egg) ------------------------------------- 28. さかな (fish)
29. えいが(movie)

Answer Key

1. toki
2. eigo
3. otoko
4. kodomo
5. kokoro
6. inu
7. kao
8. te
9. onna
10. neko
11. otousan
12. michi
13. hito
14. bangohan
15. yasai
16. hana
17. gohan
18. niku
19. tori
20. okaasan
21. mizu
22. okane
23. asagohan
24. hirugohan
25. ie
26. Nihongo

Katakana

  The flowing, rounded forms of the hiragana above were, in premodern Japan, only written by women.   Men wrote in *kanji* and the more angular *katakana*.   Of course this is no longer the case today, and the usage of *katakana* has shifted to foreign loan words, or generally words that are not Japanese. Names in languages other than Japanese and Chinese are also written in *katakana*. This explains Japanese people's sometimes curious pronunciation of English- many some in contact with English vocabulary for the first time via *katakana*, which, like *hiragana*, is much more limited in sounds than English. For example, with *n* as the only exception, words in Japanese always end in a vowel, so *cup* becomes *kappu*, *soccer* becomes *sakka*, *bus* becomes *basu*, and so on. This of course goes for English names written in Japanese as well: *George* becomes *Jooji*, *Paul* becomes *Pooru*, and so on. It's best to treat such words as distinct vocabulary; trying to pronounce them as you would in English will make your Japanese hard to understand and impair communication.

Because it's not used as often, *katakana* generally takes longer for Japanese learners to memorize than *hiragana*. However, it still appears quite ubiquitously in Japan, and will help you get a feel for how to say foreign words, your own name among them, in Japanese. The full list of *katakana* is as follows

	a	i	u	e	o	ya	yu	yo
	ア a	イ i	ウ u	エ e	オ o			
k	カ ka	キ ki	ク ku	ケ ke	コ ko	キャ kya	キュ kyu	キョ kyo
s	サ sa	シ shi	ス su	セ se	ソ so	シャ sha	シュ shu	ショ sho
t	タ ta	チ chi	ツ tsu	テ te	ト to	チャ cha	チュ chu	チョ cho
n	ナ na	ニ ni	ヌ nu	ネ ne	ノ no	ニャ nya	ニュ nyu	ニョ nyo
h	ハ	ヒ	フ	ヘ	ホ	ヒャ	ヒュ	ヒョ

	ha	hi	fu	he	ho	hya	hyu	hyo
m	マ ma	ミ mi	ム mu	メ me	モ mo	ミャ mya	ミュ myu	ミョ myo
y	ヤ ya		ユ yu		ヨ yo			
r	ラ ra	リ ri	ル ru	レ re	ロ ro	リャ rya	リュ ryu	リョ ryo
w	ワ wa				ヲ wo			
n	ン n							
g	ガ ga	ギ gi	グ gu	ゲ ge	ゴ go	ギャ gya	ギュ gyu	ギョ gyo
z	ザ za	ジ ji	ズ zu	ゼ ze	ゾ zo	ジャ ja	ジュ ju	ジョ jo
d	ダ da	ヂ* ji	ヅ dzu	デ de	ド do			
b	バ ba	ビ bi	ブ bu	ベ be	ボ bo	ビャ bya	ビュ byu	ビョ byo
p	パ pa	ピ pi	プ pu	ペ pe	ポ po	ピャ pya	ピュ pyu	ピョ pyo

Rarely used.

As in *hiragana*, a small ツ(tsu) indicates a double consonant. This is often used with katakana to reproduce the sounds of foreign words by accenting the consonant. For example, *click* is written not as クリク(kuriku) but as クリック(kurikku), which is closer to the accent of the original English word. One difference between *hiragana* and *katakana* is the way an elongated vowel is indicated. You may recall that in *hiragana* the vowel is either written twice, or in the case of an *o* or *e* sound followed by an う(u) or い(i), respectively. However, in *katakana* a dash is simply used. Some common examples include ハンバーガー(hanbaagaa / hamburger), サッカー (sakkaa / soccer), and ドーナツ(doonatsu / donut). Remember that even if this way of saying English words seems very strange at first, you'll get the hang of it the more you hear, say, and read Japanese. Soon you'll find yourself saying things the Japanese way without even realizing it! Learning this style of pronunciation can also be helpful if you ever happen to find yourself in a pinch in Japan and can't recall the vocab word you need. Let's say you need to find a hospital, but can't remember what it's called in Japanese (it's びょういん/byouin, by the way). If you ask a Japanese person where the hospital is, there's a chance you may just get a bewildered response. But if you can recall how *katakana* pronunciation works and ask for the ホスピタル(hosupitaru), you probably have a better chance of getting the directions you need. You may be surprised how much you can get by in Japanese just by pronouncing English words the Japanese way!

Practice Questions

Once you've had a chance to practice reading *katakana* and make some flashcards, try this name matching activity that will test both your *katakana* memorization as well as your ability to understand Japanese pronunciation of English words. On the left are some common English names written in *katakana*.

Try matching them with their English spelling!

1. クリス   a. Josh
2. ジョン   b. Emily
3. アレックス   c. Marcus
4. アリス   d. Catherine
5. マイケル   e. Ben
6. フアン   f. Isabella
7. ザック   g. John

8. ジェシカ   h. Zach
9. エミリー   i. Tony
10. ジョッシュ   j. Alex
11. ウィリアム   k. Jessice
12. マーカス   l. Apollo
13. ルーカス   m. Lukas
14. イザベラ   n. William
15. アポロ   o. Michael
16. トニー   p. Juan
17. キャサリン   q. Michelle
18. ミッシェル   r. Chris
19. ベン   s. Alice

Answer Key
1. r 2. g 3. j 4. s 5. o 6. p 7. h 8. k 9. b 10. a 11. n 12. c 13. m 14. f 15. l 16. i 17. d 18. q 19. e

As another exercise for your katakana Japanese, here are the names of some countries written in katakana.   See if you can guess what country they refer to.

1. オーストラリア
2. ガーナ
3. メキシコ
4. フランス
5. ブラジル
6. インドネシア
7. ベトナム
8. インド
9. ケニヤ
10. アメリカ
11. ポルトガル
12. スペイン
13. カナダ
14. ノルウェー
15. イタリア
16. オランダ
17. ロシア
18. サウジアラビア
19. ナイロビ
20. パキスタン

21. ポーランド

Answer Key

1. Australia
2. Ghana
3. Mexico
4. France
5. Brazil
6. Indonesia
7. Vietnam
8. India
9. Kenya
10. America
11. Portugal
12. Spain
13. Canada
14. Norway
15. Italy
16. Holland
17. Russia
18. Saudi Arabia
19. Nairobi
20. Pakistan
21. Poland

Although most names of countries are similar to their English names, there are some exceptions. England, for example, is called イギリス(Igirisu) in Japanese, and Germany is referred to by its German name as ドイツ(Doitsu). China and Korea have names written in *kanji,* 中国（ちゅうごく）and 韓国（かんこく）respectively, and thus do not use *katakana*. While we're talking about the names of countries it may be useful to note that adding じん (jin) to the end of the name of any country means a person from that country. So, イギリスじん is an Englishman, スペインじん is a Spaniard, and にほんじん is a Japanese person.

As mentioned earlier, your mastery of *hiragana* and *katakana* will of course not be immediate, but the more you try to read them, the more you'll notice yourself remembering. To help you in this process, this book will present problem sets written in these Japanese alphabets. Good luck, and happy memorizing!

Chapter 3: Basic Greetings (*Hi, Good Morning, Thanks*)

Greetings are given huge importance in Japanese culture. Schoolchildren are encouraged to greet their teachers and classmates actively and in a loud voice, and special school assemblies are held just to practice greeting each other. Greetings, called あいさつ (aisatsu) in Japanese, are thought to be a central part of all human interactions. When a company employee walks into the office in the morning, he or she will without fail bow and offer a hearty おはようございます(ohayou gozaimasu / good morning) to everyone else in the office, and when everyone has arrived, a morning greeting session is held when everyone will once more stand up, bow, and say おはようございます in unison again before discussing the day's business. Even if all you know of Japanese are these basic greetings, Japanese people will react much more warmly to you and greatly appreciate the effort you are making. They are the backbone of communicating in Japanese, and thus it's appropriate to learn them first.

The aforementioned おはようございます should always be how you start your day in Japanese, and we can look at it here as an example of some aspects of Japanese we'll see come up again and again. Usually exchanged until about 10 a.m., it is basically used like "good morning" in English. The final *u* in *gozaimasu* is not pronounced, so it sounds something like *o-ha-yo-o-go-za-ee-mas*, with the accent placed on the *ha*. However, like many Japanese words, its form changes depending on social context. おはようございます is a polite greeting, exchanged with strangers and superiors. For example, school principals in Japan often stand outside their school in the morning and exchange greetings with every student as they arrive at school. In this case, the principal, in his role as a superior, would say the more casual おはよう(ohayou) to his students, leaving off the ございます. The students (and other teachers for that matter) would respond with the full おはようございます. Generally, it's better to err on the side of using the more polite form unless the person you're greeting is a close friend or child. Even someone who is nominally not your superior should be greeted with a polite form until you've noticed them using the casual form with you, which means it would be appropriate for you to respond in the same way.

Other essential greetings that depend on the time of day are こんにちは (konnichiwa) and こんばんは (konbanwa). こんにちは is generally used from before noon until the evening time, and こんばんは after the evening until the night hours. One thing you may notice about these words is that the *hiragana* は is pronounced *wa*. This is an example of one of the very few exceptions in *hiragana* pronunciation. In the next chapter, we'll look more closely at other situations in which this character is pronounced in this way.

There are some other key Japanese greetings that don't have exact English counterparts. For example, いただきます(itadakimasu, again with the last *u* unpronounced) before a meal, and ごちそうさまでした（gochisousamadeshita） after a meal are absolutely essential. いただきます translates literally to "I humbly receive" and should be said with hands joined as if praying before a meal to show gratitiude. If you remember to say it even when someone just hands you a snack or a cup of tea, you'll be sure to make a good impression. ごちそうさまでした is also said with hands joined, and literally means "It was a feast," expressing gratitude for those who prepared the food.

Japanese also has specific greetings for when people are coming and going somewhere or other. Before leaving your home, you should always say いってきます(ittekimasu, *u* unpronounced), which means "I'll leave and come back," to which those staying back will respond いってらっしゃい(itterrasshai), which literally meaning "please go and come back," roughly corresponding to a "good-bye" or "take care" in English in this circumstance. When you've come back home, say ただいま（tadaima）to announce that you're back. The person or people who had been waiting for you will respond with おかえりなさい（okaerinasai）to welcome you back.

Most English speakers are familiar with the word さようなら（sayounara）, but it may not be used in the way you expect. For example, if parting with friends or family for the day, sayng またね(mata ne, or "see you again") is more typical. In a formal situation, or with someone you don't know very well, it is polite to say しつれいしました(shitsureishimashita), signifying that you are sorry for any inconvenience you might have caused them, and appreciate their time. さようなら is typically reserved for when saying good bye to someone for what will likely be an extended period of time. Think of it as a "real good bye," while an above phrase like またね would be an equivalent to "bye" or "see you."

The last greeting of the day is exchanged before going to sleep, おやすみなさい(oyasuminasai), which means "please rest," used like "good night" in English. Like おはようございます and おはよう, this phrase too can be made more casual by shortening it to おやすみ（oyasumi）.

Learning these key greetings is a huge step towards communicating effectively in Japanese, and if you can use them properly you're probably already likely to get lots of compliments from Japanese people!

Key Greetings Review

Greeting	Romaji	Meaning
おはようございます	ohayougozaimasu	Good morning
おはよう	ohayou	Good morning (casual)
こんにちは	konnnichiwa	Good Afternoon
こんばんは	konbanwa	Good Evening
いただきます	itadakimasu	(said before a meal or after receiving food or drink)
ごちそうさまでした	gochisousamadeshita	Thanks for the meal! (said after eating)
いってきます	ittekimasu	I'm going out! (said whenever leaving one's home)
いってらっしゃい	itterasshai	See you! / Take care. (said in response to いってきます)
ただいま	tadaima	I'm back
おかえりなさい	okaerinasai	Welcome back
またね	mata ne	See you! / Bye!
しつれいしました	shitsureishimashita	(Used when parting with a superior)
さようなら	sayounara	Good Bye (when parting for an extended period)
おやすみなさい	oyasuminasai	Good Night
おやすみ	oyasumi	Good Night (Casual)

Practice Questions

For each of the below situations, choose the correct greeting.

1. On a business trip to Japan, you've finished talking to a client and will now leave the room.

2. Your Japanese exchange student friend is returning to Japan, and you're saying goodbye at the airport.

3. You've walked into a small cafe to get some breakfast.

4. It's the first night of your Japanese homestay, and you're ready to go up to your room to finish unpacking and then go to sleep.

5. Some Japanese elementary school kids on the street, eager to try out some English, all say "*hello*" to you, and you in turn want to say something in Japanese to them.

6. Some Japanese business partners have visited your country and you're going out to dinner together.   You've finished eating, and want to show them you've studied some Japanese manners.

7. When you're heading out to work (a), and when you've just got back from work (b).

8. You happen to meet a friend on the street on a night out.

9. A visitor offers you a souvenir of a Japanese sweet and urges you to try it.

10. When a friend is going out to pick something up at a convenience store (a), and when they've come back (b).

11. You're saying goodbye to a classmate after a studying session.

Answer Key

1. しつれいしました
2. さようなら
3. おはようございます
4. おやすみなさい
5. こんにちは
6. ごちそうさまでした
7. (a)いってきます
7. (b)ただいま
8. こんばんは
9. いただきます
10. (a)いってらっしゃい
10. (b)おかえりなさい
11. またね

Chapter 4: It's Time To Introduce Yourself!

Any time you meet someone, whether it be in a professional, personal, educational, or in any other capacity, a self-introduction will be necessary. While learning the basics of introducing yourself, you can also familiarize yourself with some basic elements of Japanese grammar. Here we'll use the self-introduction to learn about Japanese particles as well as the immensely useful word です(desu, with the final *u* silent).

The first thing you should say when meeting someone is はじめまして (hajimemashite), roughly corresponding to "nice to meet you" in English. Next, you'll naturally want to say your name. Though there are many ways to do this, the most simple is "(your name)です." です is the Japanese equivalent of the English "be-verb," but unlike ""to be," it does not conjugate depending on person and number. Whether you're talking about yourself, another person, a tree, train, flock of seagulls, or anything else, you can use the same です. So, とりです would translate to "It/that/this is a bird;" and depending on context, カールです can mean either "He's Carl" or "I'm Carl." For greater clarity, this sentence could be elongated to "わたしのなまえはカールです," which literally means "my name is Carl." Though this phrase may seem easier to understand, native Japanese speakers in fact almost never use it. However, there are some things we can learn by analyzing this sentence.

Japanese is unique in that it has many different ways to say "I," depending on the speaker and social context. The one used here, わたし(watashi), is the most basic form, and although you'll want to start using other first-person pronouns as well if you advance in your Japanese study, using わたし is usually a safe bet for beginners. However, unlike English, sentences don't necessarily require a subject, in which case the meaning wil be inferred from the context. One of the most interesting aspects of learning Japanese is that your sense for intuiting indirect, contextual information will greatly sharpen.

Between わたし and the next word, なまえ(namae, name) we see the particle の(no). This indicates possession. In this case, わたしのなまえ means "my name." Between なまえ and カール comes the particle は. When used as a particle, like in こんにちは and こんばんは, this *hiragana* is pronounced *wa* rather than *ha,* as it would be if appearing in a word. は is called "the topic particle," and indicates the topic of the sentence, which in this case, is "my name." Broken up into words, the sentence looks like this: わたし の なまえ は カール です. As you can see, particles like は and の always come after the word they are modifying. Later we'll look at more examples of how these particles are used, but for when you are giving a simple self-introduction, just saying (your name)です is sufficient.

Next, it's a good idea to say where you're from. The word しゅっしん (shusshin) can express either home-country or home-town, so saying, for example, イギリスしゅっしんです would mean "I'm from England." As some extra information, you can say something you like as a part of your self-intro. The word for like or favorite is すき(suki, with a silent *u*). Trying this sentence out can also introduce us to another Japanese particle, が(ga). Let's say you like soccer. Of course, in English you'd say, "I like soccer," with *like* here being a verb that takes a direct object, *soccer*. However, this is expressed a little differently in Japanese. You'd say わたしはサッカーがすきです (watashi wa sakkaa ga suki desu). Here the particle が is indicating the subject of the sentence, "soccer", and は the topic, "I." Translated literally, it means something like "As for me, soccer is [my] favorite [thing]." This may seem strange to an English speaker, but if you can just remember that pattern of ___ が すきです to talk about things you or others like, you don't have to worry about the grammar so much.

Last of all may be the most important phrase of you self-introduction: よろしくおねがいします(yoroshiku onegaishimasu, again with a final silent *u*). Literally meaning something like "I humbly request that you act graciously toward me," it has no equivalent in English. It is typically used when you are requesting something or when you have first met someone. A key phrase in Japanese culture, it expresses both the debt that people have toward each other, thanks for acceptance into a group, and other complex feelings. Don't forget to finish off your introduction with this phrase!

So, in summary, you can use this as a basic template for a self-introduction:

はじめまして。-- Hajimemashite.
(your name)です。--(Your name) desu.
(your home country)しゅっしんです。----------------(Your home country) shusshin desu.
わたしは(something you like)がすきです。---------Watashi wa (something you like) ga suki desu.
よろしくおねがいします。-------------------------------Yoroshiku onegaishimasu.

Practice and master your own self-intro in Japanese!

Chapter 5: Asking Questions (Where Would We Be Without Them?)

Asking a question in Japanese is very simple. Unlike in English, the sentence's word order does not change. Simply adding か(ka) to the end is all it takes. For example, let's say you've just said わたしはサッカーがすきです, that you like soccer, and want to ask your conversation partner if he or she also likes soccer. Adding か to the end of the basic sentence will make a statement into a question: サッカーがすきです(I/you/he/she like(s) soccer) becomes サッカーがすきですか(Do you like soccer?).

Here you may feel the urge to insert the Japanese word for "you" into your question, but this raises a number of issues. Firstly, as was the case for "I," there are many different ways to say " you" in Japanese, all with very different connotations. The most standard and polite of these is あなた(anata), but even this word may sound insulting in the wrong circumstance. While it takes some getting used to, saying "you" is typically to be avoided in Japanese. Instead, use the name of the person you're speaking to. So, for the above example, if you're talking to someone named Hiroshi, instead of saying あなたはサッカーがすきですか, say ひろしさんはサッカーがすきですか, attaching the honorific さん(san) to the end of your conversation partner's name. Though many such different honorofics exist, さん is generally used with everyone except close friends.

Here are some key vocabulary and example sentences that you can use to ask a variety of questions:

Key Vocabulary

Hiragana	Romaji	Meaning
はい	hai	yes
いいえ	iie	no
そうです	sou desu	yes, that is the case, etc.
そうじゃないです	sou ja nai desu	no, that is not the case, etc.
なに/なん	nani / nan	what
だれ	dare	who
これ	kore	this
それ	sore	that (object near partner)
あれ	are	that (object distant from speaker and partner)

この	kono	this (adjective)
その	sono	that... (adjective)
あの	ano	that... (object distant from speaker and partner)
どの	dono	which...
どんな	donna	What kind of
もの	mono	thing
どうぶつ	doubutsu	animal
たべもの	tabemono	food
のみもの	nomimono	drink
くるま	kuruma	car
かばん	kaban	bag
ほん	hon	book
ふく	fuku	clothes
くつ	kutsu	shoes
めがね	megane	glasses
いろ	iro	color
あかい	akai	red
きいろ	kiiro	yellow
みどり	midori	green
あおい	aoi	blue
むらさき	murasaki	purple
しろい	shiroi	white
くろい	kuroi	black
ピンク	pinku	pink
ちゃいろ	chairo	brown
オレンジ	orenji	orange

Example Sentences

おなまえはなんですか。------ Onamae ha nan desu ka-------------------------
What's your name?

これはなんですか。------------- Kore wa nan desu ka--------------------------
What is this?

それはなんですか。------------- Sore wa nan desu ka--------------------------What is that?

かれはだれですか。------------- Kare wa dare desu ka-------------------------Who is he?

かのじょはだれですか。--------Kanojo wa dare desu ka----------------------Who is she?
ひろしさんですか。-------------Hiroshi-san desu ka-------------------------Are you Hiroshi?
どのスポーツがすきですか。-- Dono supootsu ga suki desu ka----------What sport do you like?
どんなおんがくがすきですか。-Donna ongaku ga suki desu ka--What kind of music do you like?

  The word for "what" is worth paying special attention to. Though it's standard form is なに(nani) it can be shortened to なん(nan) in the context of some question sentences. Usually when it is the subject of the sentence, it appears as なに, but when it comes directly before です, it is shortened to なん. So, for example, in the sentence なにがすきですか (what do you like?) it is not shortened, but in the sentence それはなんですか (What's that?) it is.

Answering A Question

  The standard affirmative answer to a question in Japanese is はい、そうです(hai, sou desu) or just そうです(sou desu, "yes," "that is the case," etc.). The word はい, usually translated as "yes," has a variety of uses. Not only to supply an affirmative answer to a question, it is also used as a way to indicate that you're paying attention. For example, if someone calls your name, you should respond with はい！Or, when in conversation with someone, you should frequently say はい at pauses in the conversation to indicate that you understand. Though similar to the use of "yes," "okay," or "I see" in English, this is done much more frequently in Japanese. For this reason, if you notice Japanese people saying "yes" a lot when you have a conversation with them in English, it doesn't necessarily mean that they're emphatically agreeing with every point you make, just that they're following what you're saying.

  For a negative answer, you'd say いいえ、そうじゃないです(iie, sou ja nai desu). Like はい, the word for "no," いいえ, can be used in a number of ways. It can be a show of humility when someone gives you a compliment, and also as a casual way to respond to thanks. We'll see some examples of these uses later on.

Practice Questions

Translate the following sentences from Japanese to English:

1. これはわたしのアイスクリームですか。

2. ようこのかばんはみどりですか。
3. このあかいものはなんですか。
4. あのピンクのくるまはだれのくるまですか。
5. あなたはだれですか。
6. あのしろいいぬはキムのいぬです。
7. どのいろがすきですか。
8. かのじょはむらさきのふくがすきです。
9. どののみものがすきですか。
10. あれはだれのくつですか。

Answer Key

1. Is this my ice cream?
2. Is your bag green, Yoko?
3. What's this red thing?
4. Whose is that pink car?
5. Who are you?
6. That white dog is Kim's.
7. What color do you like?
8. She likes purple clothes.
9. What drink do you like?
10. Whose shoes are those?

Chapter 6: Numbers!

Learning how to count and say numbers opens the door to several new and useful phrases you can use. Let's take a look at the basic list of numbers:

Hiragana	Romaji	Meaning
れい / ゼロ	rei / zero	zero
いち	ichi	one
に	ni	two
さん	san	three
よん	yon	four
ご	go	five
ろく	roku	six
なな	shichi	seven
はち	hachi	eight
きゅう	kyuu	nine
じゅう	juu	ten
ひゃく	hyaku	hundred
せん	sen	thousand
いちまん	ichiman	ten-thousand

From here they follow a regular pattern. Numbers in the teens are simply added onto じゅう. For example, eleven is じゅういち(juuichi), seventeen is じゅうなな(juunana), and nineteen is じゅうきゅう.(juukyuu). Bigger numbers are indicated with a numeral before じゅう, so twenty is にじゅう (nijuu), 36 is さんじゅうろく(sanjuuroku), and 78 is ななじゅうはち (nanajuuhachi). Zero can be alternatively referred to as either れい or ゼロ.

Some differences in pronunciation appear in the hundreds and thousands. Take a look at this list:

Hiragana	Romaji	Meaning
ひゃく	hyaku	one-hundred
にひゃく	nihyaku	two-hundred
さんびゃく	sanbyaku	three-hundred
よんびゃく	yonbyaku	four-hundred
ごひゃく	gohyaku	five-hundred
ろっぴゃく	roppyaku	six-hundred
ななひゃく	nanahyaku	seven-hundred

はっぴゃく	happyaku	eight-hundred
きゅうひゃく	kyuuhyaku	nine-hundred
せん	sen	thousand
にせん	nisen	two-thousand
さんぜん	sanzen	three-thousand
よんせん	yonsen	four-thousand
ごせん	gosen	five-thousand
ろくせん	rokusen	six-thousand
ななせん	nanasen	seven-thousand
はっせん	hassen	eight-thousand
きゅうせん	kyuusen	nine-thousand

Generally, a consonant following an *n* takes on it's voiced form (in other words, a " is attached), and a consonant following a く,つ, or ち is shortened to a doubling of the next consonant. However, you don't necessarily need to worry about memorizing this rule. If you can just remember the above examples, you'll start to naturally get a feel for how these words will be pronounced.

Possibly the biggest difference between Japanese and English numbers is the numeral いちまん. Although it corresponds to ten-thousand in English, saying じゅうせん would not make sense to a Japanese speaker. Instead it is treated as a new unit. Thus, twenty-thousand would be にまん(niman), 100,00 じゅうまん(juuman, literally "ten-ten-thousand) and one million ひゃくまん(hyakuman, literally one-hundred-ten-thouusand). This too takes some getting used to, but it will start to feel natural in no time once you start using numbers in Japanese.

How Old Are You?

Next, let's look at some ways we can apply this knowledge of numbers. One is a piece of information that you, dependng on personal preference, either may want to add to your self-introduction, or to keep as confidential as possible: your age. To express age in Japanese, さい is added to the end of a number. Because some exceptions similar to the ones we say above exist, let's look at the basic list:

いっさい---------issai -------------one (year old)
にさい----------- nisai -------------two (years old)
さんさい------- sansai-------------three

よんさい------- yonsai------------- four
ごさい---------- gosai -------------- five
ろくさい-------rokusai-------------six
ななさい--------nanasai----------seven
はっさい--------hassai------------eight
きゅうさい-----kyuusai--------- nine
じゅっさい------jussai ------------ten

Most reading this book are probably over ten years old, but you can adjust these to fit your age by tacking them onto the end of a basic number like にじゅう or さんじゅう. To ask how old someone else is (and it should go without saying you want to be careful who you ask this to!) you can say なんさいですか (nansai desu ka). Considering Japanese people's generally youthful appearances, you may be surprised by the answer!

What Time Is It?

Being able to ask, tell, and understand the time is also essential. To express the hour, じ(ji, written 時 in *kanji,* meaning "time") is added to the end of a number. The only irregular examples are よじ(yoji, four o'clock, yon becomes yo) and くじ(kuji, nine o'clock, kyuu is shortened to ku). In Japan, a 24-hour clock is often used, so what would be 6 pm in English becomes じゅうはちじ(juuhachiji, 18 o'clock), and midnight れいじ (reiji, zero o' clock). However, a.m. and p.m. times can also be used. In this case, a.m. is called ごぜん(gozen) and p.m. is called ごご(gogo). Minutes are expressed with the ending ふん, which takes the following forms:

いっぷん-----------ippun---------one (minute)
にふん-------------nifun-----------two (minutes)
さんぷん--------sanpun---------three
よんぷん--------yonfun----------four
ごふん-----------gofun------------five
ろっぷん-------roppun-----------six
ななふん-------nanafun--------seven
はっぷん--------happun--------eight
きゅうふん------kyuufun------nine
じゅっぷん-----juppun---------ten

Next, let's think of a real life situation. You've got a train to catch at 3:30, but you've forgotten your watch and want to know how much you need to hurry to the station. You're starting to get worried, and decide to ask a friendly-looking passerby. In this situation, the following diaolouge would be a good model to follow:

A: すみません！いまは、なんじですか。
    (sumimasen　ima　wa nanji desu ka)

B: いまはさんじにじゅうななふんです。
    (ima wa sanji juunanafun desu)

A: そうですか！ありがとうございます！
    (sou desu ka　arigatou gozaimasu)

B: どういたしまして。
    (douitashimashite)

(English)
A: Excuse me! What time is it now?
B: Now it's 3:27.
A: I see! Thank you very much!
B: You're welcome.

    First, you'll want to say すみません(sumimasen). This very useful word can be used like both "I'm sorry" and "Excuse me" in English. Generally, whenever you speak out to someone you don't know, you should say すみません first both to get their attention and apologize for taking their time. Next is the word for now, いま(ima), which is marked as the topic of the sentence by the particle は, and the question sentence なんじですか(what time is it?).

    After you've been told the time, it's appropriate to say そうですか(sou desu ka). This ubiquitous phrase can be roughly translated to "I see," and literally means something more like "Is that so?" It appears so frequently in Japanese that it's not uncommon to overhear a formal Japanese phone conversation consisting at least 50% of そうですか. Basically, anytime your conversation partner has said something you didn't know, it's appropriate to say this word.

    Next, of course, you'll want to say " thank you." There are a few ways in Japanese to do this. The most formal and polite is どうもありがとうございます(doumo arigatou gozaimasu, with silent *u*). The one used here leaves off the どうも, and is the most standard. For a more casual expression, you can just say ありがとう. The most casual of all thanks is simply saying どうも, and would be appropriate for a time like when a friend has passed you a dish.

Lastly, your conversation partner will reply with どういたしまして, which means "you're welcome."   You may remember that you can also respond to an ありがとう by saying いいえ, which is like saying "No, it's nothing." in English.

Practice Questions

Translate the following Japanese numbers into English.

1. にじゅうろく	9. はっぴゃくはちじゅう
2. さんじゅうなな	10. きゅうまんはっせん
3. きゅうひゃくにじゅうさん	11. さんじゅうまんよんせん
4. よんせんにひゃく	12. ろくじゅうにまん
5. いちまんごせんまん	13. ひゃくさんじゅうろく
6. さんまんざんぜんろっぴゃくごじゅうに	14. にじゅうきゅうまん
7. さんびゃくにじゅうよん	15. ろっぴゃくに
8. ごじゅういち	16. さんぜんよんびゃく

Choose the most correct response if said the following:
1. どうも。

a. どういたしまして
b. はい   c. そうです
d. ななじゅう

2. わたしはベトナムしゅっしんです。

a. ありがとう
b. わたしはアメリカしゅっしんです
c. おはよう
d. そうですか

3. すみません。いまはなんじですか。

a. よんぷんです

b. くじです
c. そうですか
d. ありがとう

4. なんさいですか。

a. にじゅうです。
b. にじゅうじです。
c. にじゅうさいです。
d. にじゅっぷんです。

5. わたしはよんじゅうにさいです。

a. ありがとう
b. そうです
c. そうですか
d. よんじゅっぷんですか

Answer Key

1. 26   2. 37   3. 923   4. 4200   5. 15,000   6. 33,652   7. 324   8. 51   9. 980
10. 98,000   11. 30,400   12. 620,000 13. 1,360,000   14. 290,000   15. 602   16. 3400
1. a   2. d   3. b   4. c   5. c

Chapter 7: "*What Are You Doing?*" An Introduction to Verbs

Japanese as a language is structured to fit its social context, and the hierarchical, mannered structure of Japanese society is mirrored in its grammar. This can be seen in how Japanese verbs work. Every verb has a casual form, also referred to as its "dictionary form," because this is the form used to introduce the word to a new learner, as well as various increasingly complex levels of polite forms, some that even many native Japanese aren't comfortable using. For the majority of situations you will encounter, the dictionary form and the polite *-masu* form will be sufficient. The latter is the verbal equivalent to the です sentence structure we've used until now.

Ru-verbs

Verbs that end in る tend to be the easiest to conjugate, so we'll start by working with them. Some we can try using right away appear in the below list:

Key Vocabulary

でかける	dekakeru	to go out, leave the house
つける	tsukeru	to turn on (such as a light switch)
おしえる	oshieru	to teach
はじめる	hajimeru	to begin (transitive)
みる	miru	to see, watch, look
いる	iru	to be (used for animate objects)
ねる	neru	to sleep
おきる	okiru	to wake up
あさ	asa	morning
ひる	hiru	noon, daytime
よる	yoru	evening
きょう	kyou	today
あした	ashita	tomorrow
まいにち	mainichi	everyday
ぼく	boku	I (used by male speakers)
よく	yoku	often
あまり	amari	not often, not much
でも	demo	but
から	kara	because, so

First, let's look at an example dialogue using the verb たべる(taberu, to eat) to get used to how a casual conversation with verbs works.

たけし：ジョンさんは、すしがすき？
ジョン：いいえ。わたしはさかなをたべない。
たけし：さかなをたべない？ぼくはまいにちたべる。にくは？
ジョン：いいえ、にくもたべない。わたしはベジタリアンだ。
たけし：そうですか！

Takeshi: John, do you like sushi?
John: No, I don't eat fish.
Takeshi: You don't eat fish? I eat it every day. How about meat?
John: No, I don't eat meat either. I'm a vegetarian.
Takeshi: I see!

Note that Takeshi refers to himself not with わたし, but with ぼく (boku), which is another first-person pronoun commonly used by males. Generally it's not impolite for a male to use ぼく instead of わたし if he prefers, but females rarely use it, preferring わたし instead. Because this is a casual conversation, the dictionary form of the verb たべる is used. The negative form of the verb, たべない(tabenai), also appears. In the case of たべる, dropping the る and adding ない changes the meaning from "eat" to "not eat."

There are some other important new details that may not be as easy to notice. Two new particles appear, を(wo, read as *o*) and も(mo). を is a direct object particle, and indicates the target of the action of the verb. Although written with the *hiragana* for *wo,* this particle is always read as *o* (together with the *wa* reading for は, one of the very few examples of irregular *hiragana* pronunciation). も means *also*, and takes the place of は or を when there is repetition. For example,

わたしはピザーをたべる。ステーキもたべる。
(I eat pizza. I also eat steak.)

In addition to these particles, John declares himself a vegetarian not by saying ベジタリアンです, but ベジタリアンだ. This is because だ is the casual form of です. From this conversation, we can presume that John and Takeshi are friends, and so don't need to worry about using polite language. However, Takeshi simply asks すしがすき？ instead of すしがすきですか.

This is because the か particle does not follow the casual だ- in this case all it takes to make a question is a risen intonation on the end of the sentence.

For our next example, we'll look at a situation you may encounter- being presented with a food you're totally unfamiliar with, and, if you don't have the most adventurous of pallates, may not want to eat. The setting here is a more formal dinner party, so polite language will be used.

ジョン：すみません。あのあかいものはなんですか。
めぐみ：これはいくらです。たべますか。
ジョン：いくらはなんですか。
めぐみ：さかなのたまごです。
ジョン：すみません。たべません・・・・

John: Excuse me. What is this red stuff?
Megumi: It's *ikura*.   Would you like some?
John: What's *ikura*?
Megumi: It's fish eggs.
John: Sorry. No thanks...

Here the dictionary form たべる was changed into its polite -masu (silent *u*) form by dropping the る and adding *masu*, or *masen* for the negative form.

While reading some example sentences using these words, see if you can identify the two new particle that appears in some of them and guess its meaning!

わたしはレストランにでかける。
I'm going to go to a restaurant.

たなかさんはぼくににほんごをおしえます。
Mr. Tanaka teaches me Japanese.

いまにほんにいません。カナダにいます。
I'm not in Japan now. I'm in Canada.

まいにちじゅうにじにねます。ろくじにおきます。
Every day I go to bed at 12. I wake up at six.

ひるはステーキをたべる。よるにもステーキをたべる。
I'm going to eat steak in the afternoon, and again in the evening.

ぼくはサッカーがすきだから、よくテレビでみる。
I like soccer, so I often watch it on TV.

レストランがすき。でも、あまりいかない。
I like restaurants, but I don't go to them very often.

きょうはたけしのいえでねる。
I'll sleep at Takeshi's house today.

      The new particles are に(ni) and で(de), and both have to do with position and location in some way. に acts as an indirect object particle or as an indicator of direction, standing in for such words as *to, in,* and *for* in English. It can also be used to indicate the time at which something is done. で indicates the place at which something is done. For example, レストランにいく would mean "go to a restaurant," while レストランでたべる would mean " eat at a restaurant." で can also be used to express means. In the above example, watching something on TV is expressed by "テレビでみる." Once you've learned some more verbs you'll see many more examples of all of these uses appear again and again.

      でも and から are two more very common words that are worthy of extra explanation. Unlike the English *but*, which usually is not used to start a sentence, the Japanese でも never comes in the middle of a sentence. So, for example, it would be correct to say サーモンがすきです。でも、ツナがすきじゃないです (I like salmon, but I don't like tuna), but incorrect to say サーモンがすきでも、ツナがすきじゃないです。から、on the other hand, always follows the casual form of a verb or the casual ending だ, even in a polite sentence. When it comes at the beginning of a new sentence, it is instead written as だから. Here's some examples of each of these uses:

まいにちよるのさんじにねるから、あさにおきません。
I go to sleep at 3 in the morning everyday, so I don't get up in the morning.

わたしはにほんじんだから、えいごをおしえません。
I'm Japanese, so I don't teach English.

きょうスターウォーズ'をみる、だから、よるにでかけない。
I'm watching Star Wars today, so I won't be going out tonight.

Looking at these sentences, you may be wondering about the tense and person of these verbs. However, these are much more ambiguous in Japanese than in English. A verb does not change depending on whether the subject is singular or plural, and the Japanese language often doesn't even need to make this distinction. This ambiguous, more impressionistic take on communication can take some getting used to, but it will open up a new sense and way of thinking to you. Also, verbs in these forms can refer to either habitually performed actions or actions to be performed in the future. We'll look at ways to express other tenses in the coming chapters.

Practice Questions

Change each word in casual form to its polite form, and vice versa.

1. でかけない 2. たべる 3. みます 4. ねません 5. はじめない 6. おしえません 7. います

Choose the correct word or particle to fit in each blank, then translate the sentence.

1. きょうプロジェクト＿はじめる＿、ねない。

2. あなた＿にほん＿アニメ＿みますか。

3. まいにちいえ＿インスタントヌードル＿たべる。＿、すきじゃない。

4. きょうがっこう＿えいが＿みる。

5. はちじ＿クラブ＿でかける。

6. わたしはにほん＿ドラマ＿みる。かんこく＿ドラマ＿みる。

Answer Key
1. でかけません
2. たべます
3. みる
4. ねない
5. はじめません
6. おしえない
7. いる

1. を、から

Because I'm starting the project today, I won't get any sleep.

2. は、の、を
Do you watch Japanese anime?

3. で、を、でも
Everyday I eat instant noodles at home, but I don't like it.

4. で、を
We'll watch a movie today at school.

5. に、に
I'm going out to a club at eight.

6. の、を、の、も
I watch Japanese dramas. I also watch Korean dramas.

U-Verbs

The verbs looked at in the previous chapter ("ru-verbs") are the eastiest to conjugate, but there are also verbs that change in a slightly different way.   Take a look at the following list and see if you can catch on to what the difference is.

Dictionary Form	Polite Form	Meaning
あう　(au)	あいます　(aimasu)	to meet
いう　(iu)	いいます　(iimasu)	to say
うたう　(utau)	うたいます　(utaimasu)	to sing
かう　(kau)	かいます　(kaimasu)	to buy
いく　(iku)	いきます　(ikimasu)	to go
あるく　(aruku)	あるきます　(arukimasu)	to walk
かく　(kaku)	かきます　(kakimasu)	to write
きく　(kiku)	ききます　(kikimasu)	to hear
およぐ　(oyogu)	およぎます　(oyogimasu)	to swim
はなす　(hanasu)	はなします　(hanashimasu)	to speak
まつ　(matsu)	まちます　(machimasu)	to wait
もつ　(motsu)	もちます　(mochimasu)	to have, to hold
あそぶ　(asobu)	あそびます　(asobimasu)	to play
とぶ　(tobu)	とびます　(tobimasu)	to jump, to fly
のむ　(nomu)	のみます　(nomimasu)	to drink

よむ (yomu)	よみます (yomimasu)	to read
ある (aru)	あります (arimasu)	to be (for inanimate objects)
うる (uru)	うります (urimasu)	to sell
おわる (owaru)	おわります (owarimasu)	to end
かえる (kaeru)	かえります (kaerimasu)	to return, come back
つくる (tsukuru)	つくります (tsukurimasu)	to make
はいる (hairu)	はいります (hairimasu)	to enter
わかる (wakaru)	わかります (wakarimasu)	to understand
する (suru)	します (shimasu)	to do

As you can see, these verbs change to the polite form by changing the final *u* sound of the dictionary form to an *i* before adding ます, unlike ru-verbs, which simple drop the final る. The most difficult is differentiating verbs of this type (called *u-verbs*) that end in る in the dictionary form from *ru-verbs*. For example, seeing that the verb for "to begin" changes from the casual form はじめる to the polite form はじめます, you may assume that the verb for "to end," おわる, becomes おわます, but the correct form is おわります. Thus, in the beginning stage, it's best to memorize these verbs according to their -masu form.

Japanese has a very small number of irregular verbs, and one of them is the word for "to do," する. This word can be widely used. For example, "to play soccer" would be called "サッカーをする" (the verb translated as "to play" above is used in the sense of children's play or leisure activities, rather than to play a sport or instrument. As an exception to the rule, this verb becomes します in the polite form.

The negative form of these verbs also differs from those introduced in the previous section:

Negative Form

Dictionary Form	Polite Form	Meaning
あわない (awanai)	あいません (aimasen)	not meet
いわない (iwanai)	いいます (iimasen)	not say
うたわない (utawanai)	うたいません (utaimasen)	not sing

かわない (kawanai)	かいません (kaimasen)	not buy
いかない (ikanai)	いきません (ikimasen)	not go
あるかない (arukanai)	あるきません (arukimasen)	not walk
かかない (kakanai)	かきません (kakimasen)	not write
きかない (kikanai)	ききません (kikimasen)	not hear
およがない (oyoganai)	およぎません (oyogimasen)	not swim
はなさない (hanasanai)	はなしません (hanashimasen)	not speak
またない (matanai)	まちません (machimasen)	not wait
もたない (motanai)	もちません (mochimasen)	not have, hold
あそばない (asobanai)	あそびません (asobimasen)	not play
とばない (tobanai)	とびません (tobimasen)	not jump, fly
のまない (nomanai)	のみません (nomimasen)	not drink
よまない (yomanai)	よみません (yomimasen)	not read
ない (nai)	ありません (arimasen)	not (for inanimate objects)
うらない (uranai)	うりません (urimasen)	not sell
おわらない (owaranai)	おわりません (owarimasen)	not end
かえらない (kaeranai)	かえりません (kaerimasen)	not return, come back
つくらない (tsukuranai)	つくりません (tsukurimasen)	not make
はいらない (hairanai)	はいりません (hairimasen)	not enter
わからない (wakaranai)	わかりません (wakarimasen)	not understand

In the casual form, the final *u* sound becomes *a,* and ない is attached. One exception to this rule is that verbs ending in う change to わ rather than あ. For the polite form, simply replace ます with ません. Another exception is the verb ある, the negative form for which is ない. To get a feel for how this and the similar verb いる work, read these example sentences.

Key Vocabulary & Meaning

ドア (doa) --door
まど (mado) --window
つくえ (tsukue) ------------------------------------desk
そば (soba) ---near
となり (tonari) -------------------------------------next to
した (shita) --under
なか (naka) --inside
うえ (ue) ---on, above
どこ (doko) --where (question word)

いましおださんはいません。
Mr. Shioda is currently not present.

ぼくのいえはペットがいない。
I don't have any pets in my house.

まどのそばにはながある。
There's a flower next to the window.

ぼくはおかねがない。
I don't have any money.

このかばんのなかにわたしのほんがある。
My books are in this bag.

わたしのペンはロバートのつくえのしたにある？
Is my pen under your desk, Robert?

      As you can see in the above examples, the verbs いる and ある always take the に particle, and words expressing location use the particle の, "a cat in a bag" would be called かばんのなかのねこ, and the full sentence "a cat is in the bag" かばんのなかにねこがいる. These verbs can also be used to express whether something is present or not, or whether or not someone has something using は for the place or owner, and が for the item in question, as illustrated in the above sentences "ぼくのいえはペットがいない" ("I don't have any money," literally something like "As for me, there is no money") and "ぼくのいえはペットがいない" ("I don't have any pets in my house," literally "As for my house, there are no pets.")

Once you've practiced these new words, try some challenge questions to check your comprehension of how u-verbs work.

Practice Questions

Change the following verbs in positive form to negative, and vice versa:

1. おわらない 2. はいります 3. うる 4. かう 5. あいません 6. ある

Change the following verbs from casual to polite form, and vice versa:

1. かえる 2. もちます 3. よむ 4. いわない 5. つくります 6. まつ

Choose the correct word or particle to fit in each blank, then translate the sentence.

1．にほんご＿わからない。＿、にほん＿いく。

2．A: ぼく＿ビール＿どこですか。
　　B: テーブル＿うえ＿あります。

3．おとおさん＿こども＿テレビゲーム＿あそびます。

4．A: どんなおんがく＿すきですか。
　　B: わたし＿ジャズ＿ききます。

Answer Key

1. わかる 2. はいりません 3. うらない 4. かわない 5. あいます 6. ない

1.かえります 2、もつ 3．よみます 4．いいません 5．つくる 6．まちます

1．を、でも、に
I don't understand Japanese, but I'm going to Japan.

2．の、は、の、に
A: Where's my beer?
B: It's on the table.

3. も、も、で
Dad as well as the kids play video games.

4. が、は、を
A: What kind of music do you like?
B: I listen to jazz.

Chapter 8: Hey, Let's Go Shopping!

Japan's urban areas are shopping paradises, with everything from truly labyrinthine, seemingly never-ending department stores to specialized shopping districts catering to everything from tatami mats to maid costumes. Especially in one of Japan's big city's like Tokyo or Osaka, the only limits to the shopping you can do are your time, wallet, and imagination. To take a dip inside that world, it definitely helps to be armed with some Japanese.

What Do You Want?

When shopping in Japan, the first thing you'll without a doubt notice is the astounding level of service. Japanese employees are always focused, intent, and absolutely dedicated to helping the customer in absolutely any way they can. However, many will likely be shy or hesitant to use English. Even a little bit of Japanese from your end will go a long way.

The first thing you'll hear upon entering any kind of store at any time of day, whether it be a convenience store, high class restaurant, fashion parlor, barbor shop, or anything else is いらっしゃいませ (irasshaimase). Literally translating to "Please come in," you may find it curious that employees will continue saying this even long after you've entered the store. It's essentially a way for the employee to acknowledge your presence and make it clear they're ready to serve you. However, unless you plan on working in the Japanese service industry, this isn't necessarily a word you need to know how to say. The following words may be more helpful to you:

Key Vocabulary & Meaning

ほしい (hoshii) --want
あたらしい (atarashii) --------------------------------------new
ふるい (furui) --old
おいしい (oishii) --delicious
おおきい (ookii) ---big
ちいさい (chiisai) ---small
おもしろい (omoshiroi) ------------------------------------interesting
かわいい (kawaii) ---cute
ながい (nagai) ---long
みじかい (mijikai) ---short
むずかしい (muzukashii) ----------------------------------difficult
やさしい (yasashii) --easy, kind
いい (ii) ---good

わるい (warui) ---------- bad
たかい (takai) ---------- high, expensive
やすい (yasui) ---------- cheap
あつい (atsui) ---------- hot
さむい (samui) ---------- cold
いくら (ikura) ---------- how much (question word)
おつり (otsuri) ---------- change (money)
ください (kudasai) ---------- please
おかし (okashi) ---------- snacks
みせる (miseru) ---------- show
みせ (mise) ---------- store
ほしい (hoshii) ---------- want
どう (dou) ---------- how (question word)
えん (en) ---------- yen (Japanese currency)
ちょっと (chotto) ---------- a little
もっと (motto) ---------- more

Example Dialogue

くみこ：いらっしゃいませ！
メアリー：すみません。このみせは、ドレスがありますか。
くみこ：あります。どんなドレスがほしいですか。
メアリー：かわいいものがいいです。
くみこ：そうですか。あります。
メアリー：みせてください。
くみこ：これはどうですか。
メアリー：それがほしいです。いくらですか。
くみこ：きゅうせんえんです。
メアリー：はい。いちまんえん。
くみこ：おつりはせんえんです。ありがとうございました。

Kumiko: Welcome!
Mary: Excuse me. Does this shop have dresses?
Kumiko: Yes, we do.   What kind of dress would you lke?
Mary: Something cute would be nice.
Kumiko: I see. We have that.
Mary: Please show me.
Kumiko: How's this?
Mary: I'd like that. How much is it?

Kumiko: 9000 yen.
Mary: Okay. Here's 10,000 yen.
Kumiko: Your change is 1000 yen. Thank you very much!

One new key word that appears in this dialogue is ほしい, which is used to indicate what one wants. However, rather than acting as a verb, like it does in English, and taking the direct object particle を, it acts like すき and takes the subject particle が. So, for example, "I want cola" would be "コーラがほしい," and in this dialogue the question "what kind of dress do you want" is rendered as どんなドレスがほしいですか." It should also be noted that this word can act like an adjective. Japanese adjectives always come before the word they modify, and adjectives ending in い, like all of those presented above, require no modification. We saw this use before in regards to colors. So, a long book would be "ながいほん," a cute cat a "かわいいねこ," a blue shirt an "あおいシャツ、" and a game that one wants a "ほしいゲーム."

Some key phrases you'll definitely want to remember that we see here are the indispensable "いくらですか" (how much is it?) and "これはどうですか" (how's this [one]?). While deals certainly exist if you look in the right places, Japanese goods, while of a very high quality, can tend to be expensive. Here Mary doesn't mind paying 9000 yen for her dress, but if you want something a little cheaper, phrases like "もっとやすいものがありますか" (Do you have anything cheaper?) and "ちょっとたかいです" (That's a little expensive) will come in handy. As you may be able to guess, Japanese sizes tend to run a little small. Thus, you can use the same pattern to say things like "これはちょっとちいさいです" (This is a little small) or "もっとおおきいものがありますか" (Do you have anything bigger?).

The main new grammar point we see in this passage is the phrase "みせてください", translated as "please show me." To make a request of someone, something called the *te-form* of the verb is combined with the word ください. The way that verbs morph into the *te-form* depends on the ending of their dictionary form:

Dictionary Form & Te-form

たべる (taberu) --たべて (tabete)
いう (iu) ---いって (itte)
きく (kiku) --きいて (kiite)
およぐ (oyogu) --およいで (oyoide)
はなす (hanasu) ---はなして (hanashite)

まつ (matsu) --- まって (matte)
あそぶ (asobu) -- あそんで (asonde)
のむ (nomu) -- のんで (nonde)
ある (aru) -- あって (atte)
おわる (owaru)-- おわって (owatte)
する (suru) --- して (shite)

In summary, ru-verbs simply drop their last syllable and replace it with て, verbs ending in う with って, く with いて, ぐ with いで, す with して, つ with って, ぶ with んで, む with んで, る (u-verbs ending in る) with って, and our irregular verb する becomes して. This surely seems like a random and confusing batch of information to memorize, but like many such aspects of Japanese or any language, the more you practice, listen to, and use these words, you'll be able to produce te-forms without thinking twice. In addition to the command / request use we see here, the te-form has many, many uses, so you'll use it nearly constantly, and thus catch on to its sound quickly. There is only one exception to this pattern, and it is the verb いく, "to go." While it would seem to become いいて, it's te-form is in fact いって. Other than this one rare case, all regular verbs will follow the above patterns.

The te-form on its own is a curt, direct command. You definitely want to be careful about using this form, as it can sound quide rude in the wrong situation. It's better to attach ください to the end of the form, somewhat softening the command and making it more polite. Using two common phrases to illustrate this example, "ちょっとまって" can be translated to "wait a minute!" while "ここでまってください" to "please wait here." While reviewing the verbs introduced in the last chapter, try to think of what phrase would be appropriate to use in the following situations:

1. You friend bought a new CD you're interested in, and you want to see it.
2. A visitor has showed up and keeps standing outside your door, and you want to welcome them in.
3. Your shy friend is being a little reticient about some interesting gossip over dinner, and you want to hear more.
4. You're at karaoke, and it's your boyfriend / girlfriend's turn to sing.
5. You've just met some business partners, and they request a document you realize you left in another room.
6. At a business dinner, the man sitting next to you seems like he'd like to order another beer, but isn't sure whether it would be appropriate or not.
7. You're hungry and want your friend to go pick up some food for you.

Change the following verbs from their dictionary forms to their te-forms:

1. いう
2. はなす
3. わかる
4. とぶ
5. たべる
6. のむ
7. かう
8. うる
9. おわる
10. はじめる

Answer Key

(Keep in mind that there are variations on how you could word these phrases, and just because your answer isn't exactly the same as this one doesn't necessarily mean you're wrong.)

1. あたらしいCD（シーディー）をみせて！
2. はいってください。
3. もっとはなしてください！
4. うたって！
5. すみません、ちょっとまってください。
6. もっとビールをのんでください。
7. おいしいものをかってください。

1.いって　2. はなして　3. わかって　4. とんで　5. たべて　6. のんで　7. かって　8. うって　9. おわって　10. はじめて

Chapter 9: Are *You* Hungry? Looking for a Restaurant...

Getting There (Or Anywhere)

The idea of going to a Japanese restaurant may seem both exciting and overwhelming. Japan, especially in its urban areas, offers nearly every kind of cuisine imaginable if you look, but the most common genres are called ようしょく (western food, usually consisting of things like curry, hamburger steak, omelets, etc.), ちゅうかりょうり (Chinese food) and, of course, わしょく (Japanese food). However, within each of these categories, restaurants tend to be highly diversified. Unlike those in some other countries, Japanese establishments, especially those specializing in Japanese food, tend to focus on variations of only one dish. For example, a sushi restaurant would only sell sushi, an udon restaurant only udon, a ramen restaurant only ramen, etc.

To express the name of this kind of speciality shop, just add や to the end of the name of the food: so if you're hungry for some sushi, you'll want to ask someone where a すしや is. Japanese people are generally very eager to help foreign visitors to their country (to the extent that some may approach you and insist on offering you some kindof help before you even ask for it!) so if you can ask someone using this Japanese, whether it be a passerby on the street or someone working in one of the convenience stores that seem to be on every corner, you're likely to get the directions you need, especially considering that, owing to the density of Japanese streets, whatever you're looking for often tends to only be a couple of blocks away. Let's take this on as our challenge: you're wandering the streets at night, hankering for some ramen. Not content to follow some boring tourist guidebook, if you decide to take matters into your own hands and ask a friendly-looking old man sitting nearby for help, armed with the below vocab and grammar, your conversation may end up looking like the following dialogue.

Key Vocabulary	Meaning
みぎ (migi)	right
ひだり (hidari)	left
まっすぐ (massugu)	straight
うしろ (ushiro)	back
つぎ (tsugi)	next (takes the の particle)
かど (kado)	corner
しんごう (shingou)	streetlight
さがす (sagasu)	look for
とおる (tooru)	pass
わかりました (wakarimashita)	Understood, I got it

きのう (kinou) --yesterday

Sample Dialogue

A: すみません。おいしいラーメンやをさがしています。
B: ラーメンや？そうか。このみちにまっすぐいって、つぎのかどにみぎにまがって、そのつぎのしんごうをとおります。ひだりにラーメンやがあります。
A: すみません。もういちどいってください。
B: まっすぐにいって、つぎかどにみぎにまがります。つぎのしんごうをとおって、ラーメンやはひだりにあります。
A: そうですか。みぎにまがって、しんごうをとおって、ひだりですか。わかりました。ありがとうございます。
B: いいえ！

A: Excuse me. I'm looking for a good ramen shop.
B: Ramen? Let's see. Go straight down this street, turn right at the next corner, and pass the street light. There will be a ramen shop on the left.
A: I'm sorry. Could you say it one more time?
B: Go straight, and turn at the next right. Pass the next streetlight, and there's a ramen shop on the left.
A: I see. Turn left, pass the street light, on the left. Got it. Thank you very much!
B: No problem!

This short but super-useful dialogue is packed with new grammar and terms, so let's look at them one by one.

Present Progressive Verbs

Until now we've dealt with verbs in their dictionary forms, which express action done habitually or in the future. However, in the sentence "おいしいラーメンやをさがしています," the speaker is currently, at that very moment, searching for the ramen shop. For actions currently being performed (expressed by the be-verb + -ing in English), the -ている form is used. For any verb, simply add いる (or います for the polite form) to the te-form. Some examples:

いまサッカーしています。ロンさんもしますか。
We're playing soccer now. Would you like to play too, Ron?

いまばんごはんをたべているから、はなさない。
I'm eating dinner right now, so I can't talk.

にほんごでいっているから、わからない。
He's speaking in Japanese, so I can't understand.

Multiple Verbs

The te-form can also be used to connect multiple verbs in a single sentence. Some examples of this use:

きょうがっこうにいって、いえにかえって、えいがをみる。
Today I'm going to go to school, then come home and watch a movie.

わたしはピラフをつくってたべます。ひろしさんもたべますか。
I'm going to make and eat some pilaf.   Would you like to eat some too, Hiroshi?

Past Tense Verbs

In this dialogue, the speaker says "わかりました" (wakarimashita) after he or she has confirmed the directions.   This is an important word to remember, as it's how you signify to your conversation partner that you've understood the information conveyed.   Literally meaning, "I understood," it is the past tense form of わかりました.   As you can tell, verbs are changed to the past-tense in the polite form by changing the final ます to ました.   In the casual form, the verb changes similarly to the te-form, but the て is replaced with た.   Some examples:

Dictionary Form	Casual Past Tense	Polite Past Tense	Meaning
でかける	でかけた (dekaketa)	でかけました (dekakemashita)	went out
はなす	はなした (hanashita)	はなしました (hanashimashita)	talked
あそぶ	あそんだ (asonda)	あそびました (asobimashita)	played
よむ	よんだ (yonda)	よみました (yomimashita)	read
もつ	もった (motta)	もちました (mochimashita)	held, had
およぐ	およいだ (oyoida)	およぎました (oyogimashita)	swam
かえる	かえった (kaetta)	かえりました	returned

		(kaerimashita)	
する	した (shita)	しました (shimashita)	did

As a bonus, here's a list of various Japanese words that will allow you to ask for directions to other places as well:

びょういん (byouin) ---hospital
とこや (tokoya) ---barber shop
スーパー (suupaa) ---supermarket
コンビニ (konbini) ---convenience store
ほんや (honya) ---book store
ホテル (hoteru) ---hotel
こうばん (kouban) ---polite station
ゆうびんきょく (yuubinkyoku) ---post office
ぎんこう (ginkou) ---bank

Practice Questions

Change the following words to the past tense:

1. わかります
2. おわる
3. かう
4. うります
5. よむ
6. します
7. とぶ
8. まちます
9. きく
10. かきます

Translate the following sentences:

1. きょうスーパーにいって、サーモンをかいました。
2. プールにはいって、レモネードをのむ。
3. あたらしいほんをよんだ？
4. おんがくをきくから、わたしのヘッドフォンをさがしてください。テーブルのしたにある。
5. A: なにをしていますか。

B:トイレをさがしています。
6. たかいものをもっていない。
7. キミさんはそのピザをつくりましたか。
8. えいがをみて、ねました。
9. わたしのいえをとおりましたか。
10. コンビニにいって、コーラをかってください。

Answer Key

1. わかりました
2. おわった
3. かった
4. うりました
5. よんだ
6. しました
7. とんだ
8. まちました
9. きいた
10. かきました

1. Today I went to the supermarket and bought salmon.
2. I'm gonna get in the pool and drink lemonade.
3. Did you read the new book?
4. I'm gonna listen to music, so can you look for my headphones? They're under the table.
5. A: What are you doing?
   B: I'm looking for a bathroom.
6. I don't have any expensive things.
7. Did you make that pizza, Kimi?
8. I watched the movie and fell asleep.
9. Did you pass my house?
10. Could you please go to a convenience store and buy a cola?

Making An Order

So let's say you've arrived at the restaurant. Depending on what kind of place it is, there are a few possible variations as to how things will go down. If you're in Tokyo, because of the extreme density of space, many noodle shops are designed for the customers to eat while standing up. It may not be something you're used to, but it's sure to be a non-touristy, authentically Japanese experience if you challenge this kind of establishment! If you do, there's probably no menu, and if you try to order from the cook after stepping in, you're likely to be met with confusion. This is because either outside the shop or near the door there's a ticket machine, into which you insert your money, press the button for the food you want, and receive a ticket, which you'll present to the cook behind the counter. Because the ticket machine will almost surely be written in all Japanese, this is where your *hiragana* and *katakana* skills will serve you. Even if you're not completely sure what everything is, it's probably all delicious, so follow your gut instincts and try what sounds good!

If you're looking for something a little simpler, a sit down restaurant may be a better choice. One convenient aspect of Japanese menus is that almost always pictures of all the menu items will be posted, so even if you can't read some *kanji* on the menu, you can just point to what you want. Let's look at how an exchange in a restaurant may proceed:

A:　いらっしゃいませ。メニューです。
B:　ありがとうございます。
　・・・
B:　(Pointing to picture on the menu)　これはなんですか。
A:　それはおやこどんです。
B:　おやこどんはなんですか。
A:　とりにくとたまごとごはんです。
B:　そうですか。おやこどんをください。
A:　わかりました。まってください。

A: Welcome.　Here's our menu.
B: Thank you.
…
B: What is this?
A: It's *oyakodon*.
B: What's *oyakodon*?
A: It's chicken, eggs, and rice.
B: Okay. *Oyakodon*, please.
A: Understood. Please wait.

One new particle appears in this dialogue, と, which is used to connect nouns. Some other examples of this use:

パムとリックはダイナーにはいった。
Pam and Rick went in the diner.

ばんごはんにスパゲッティとパンをたべました。
I had spaghetti and bread for dinner.

This particle can also be used to indicate doing something together with someone or something.

たなあせんせいとはなしました。
I talked with Mr. Tanaka.

こどもはいぬとあそんだ。
The child played with a dog.

As a summary, we've learned the following particles so far:

Particle & Meaning

は-------------------------------- topic particle
の--------------------------------possessive particle
が--------------------------------subject particle (use with すき、ほしい、ある、and いる)
に--------------------------------to, for, towards, at (direction, time)
で--------------------------------at, with (location, means)
も--------------------------------also, both
と--------------------------------and

As seen in the above example, をください following a noun is used to request an item. This could also, for example, be used to buy a ticket with "きっぷをください。"

Practice Questions

Fill in the black with the appropriate word or particle, and translate the sentence:

1. うしろ＿いって、みぎ＿みてください。まんがや＿ほんや＿あります。
2. おいしいそばや＿さがしています。どこ＿ありますか。
3. このホテル＿やすいですか。ぼく＿おかね＿あまりもっていません。
4. ユーモア＿アクション＿ある＿、このえいが＿おもしろい。
5. きょうはテスト＿プロジェクト＿ある＿、むずかしい。
6. ビルさん＿えいご＿はなしました。

Answer Key

1. に、を、と、が

Go back, and look to the right.　There's a bookstore and manga shop there.

2. を、に

I'm looking for a good soba restaurant.　Where is one?

3. は、は、を

Is this hotel cheap?　I don't have a lot of money.

4. も、も、から、は

Because it's got both humor and action, this movie is interesting.

5. も、も、から

I've got a test as well as a project today, so it's difficult.

6. と、で

I talked with Bill in English.

Chapter 10: Riding the Train (You Won't Get Lost, I Promise!)

The public transportation system is one of the best things about Japan. Always on time, efficient speedy, and fun, you can get just about anywhere by train in Japan. However, in the bigger and busier stations, things can get a little confusing. Multiple tracks, hard to remember line names, and sometimes confusing time tables can catch even those who have lived in Japan for years off guard. Luckily, there are usually easily identifiable employees around who can help you. Almost anyone who comes to Japan is probably going to ride on a train, so let's prepare for a possibly sticky situation as our final challenge.

Key Vocabulary & Meaning

でんしゃ----------------------------------train
くるま--------------------------------car
えき----------------------------------station
せん------------------------------- train line (ex: やまのてせん= Yamanote Line)
〜ばんめ--------------------------------- denotes ordinal number – (ex: いちばんめ = first)
〜ゆき----------------------------------bound for-
のりば----------------------------------train platform
まどぐち----------------------------------ticket window
でいりぐち----------------------------------entrance and exit
きた----------------------------------North
みなみ----------------------------------South
にし----------------------------------West
ひがし----------------------------------East
おりる, おります----------------------------------to get off (ru-verb)
のる、のります----------------------------------to ride / to get on (u-verb)

For our example dialogue, let's imagine you're in Tokyo station, and you don't know anything except that you want to go to Shinjuku. Overwhelmed by the crowds and scope of the station, you approach an employee for help.

Example Dialogue

A:　すみません。しんじゅくにいきたいです。
B:　しんじゅくですか。やまのてせんのむさしこなげいゆきでんしゃにのります。
A:　どののりばですか。
B:　のりばななです。

A: そうですか。いついきますか。
B: さんじよんじゅっぷん。
A: どのえきにおりますか。
B: しんじゅくえき。じゅうさんばんめのえきです。
A: きっぷをどこでかいますか。
B: みなみでいりぐちのとなりのまどぐちで。
A: はい、わかりました。ありがとうございます。
B: どういたしまして。

A: Excuse me.   I want to go to Shinjuku.
B: Shinjuku? You'll ride on the Yamanote Line train bound for Musashi Konagei.
A: Where's the platform?
B: Platform 7.
A: I see. When does it leave?
B: At 3:40.
A: Which station will I get off at?
B: Shinjuku Station. It's the 13th station.
A: Where do I buy my ticket?
B: At the ticket window near the South Entrance.
A: I see. Thank you very much.
B: You're welcome.

Where Do You Want to Go?

You probably noticed that the unknown verb form いきたい appeared in the first line, and in the English translation was rendered as "want to go to." Verbs ending in たい express your desire, or something you want to do. So "ほんをよみたい" means "I want to read a book," "バレーボールをしたい" means "I want to play volleyball;" and "ピカチュウにあいたい" means "I want to meet Pikachu."   To make this form, simply drop the ます from the polite form and add たい. Remember that in polite form, です will come at the end of the sentence, while in casual form it will not.   Here are some examples of how this form is made:

Dictionary Form	Tai Form	Meaning
のむ	のみたい (nomitai)	want to drink
かえる	かえりたい (kaeritai)	want to return
たべる	たべたい (tabetai)	want to eat
おりる	おりたい (oritai)	want to get off

のる	のりたい (noritai)	want to ride on / get on
さがす	さがしたい (sagashitai)	want to look for
もつ	もちたい (mochitai)	want to have / hold

If you can commit these words and phrases to your memory, you can surely take on even Tokyo's vast railway system with confidence, and maybe even find a new hobby, riding around and around the pleasant train cars, gazing at the amazing vistas that unfold outside the window (as long as it's not rush hour that is!).

Practice Questions

What would you ask in the following situations:
1. You don't know where the ticket window is.
2. You want to go to Tokyo Sky Tree, but don't know what station to get off at.
3. The train has stopped at the station you want to get off at, but the train is very crowded and some people are blocking your way.

Translate the following sentences:

1. さけをのみたいです。このホテルにバーがありますか。
2. のりばにいって、しゅうぜんじゆきでんしゃにのってください。きゅうばんめのえき、たきょうえきにおります。
3. すみません。たべものがほしいです。レストランはどこですか。
4. ここはきたでいりぐちです。みにみぐちにポールとあうから、いまいきます。
5. なんばんめのしんごうにまがりますか。

Answer Key

1. まどぐちはどこですか。
2. とうきょうスカイーツリーにいきたいです。どこにおりますか。
3. すみません。おりたいです。

1. I want to drink some sake. Is there a bar at this hotel?
2. Go to Platform 2 and get on the train bound for Shuzenji. You'll get off at the ninth station, Takyo Station.
3. Excuse me. I want some food. Where is a restaurant?
4. This is the North Entrance. I'm meeting Paul at the South Entrance, so I'm going to go there now.
5. Which street light should I turn at?

Conclusion
Now Embark on Your Own Adventure!

If you've gotten this far, it's safe to say you're well on your way to mastering the basics of Japanese, and you're ready to take on a number of situations that could occur if you're in Japan. If you can learn all the grammar and vocabulary in this book, it's up to you where to go next. Starting to take a plunge into the world of *kanji* is a must if you wish to acquire truly advanced Japanese skills. If you're looking for simpler communication abilities, think of how you can fit these lessons to other practical situations. Whatever your goal, immersion is the key. Try listening to some Japanese music. Watch a Japanese movie in Japanese without the subtitles. It may sound crazy, but you may be surprised to find that you understand some. The more you do this kind of thing, the better your Japanese will become. This book drew the first steps of your map for you; now it's your journey. May your Japanese studies take you some where you've never experienced before, whether it be in Japan itself or within the thrill of learning a new language!

To your success,

Dagny Taggart

Preview Of "Learn Spanish In 7 DAYS! - The Ultimate Crash Course To Learn The Basics of the Spanish Language In No Time"

Are You ready? It's Time To Learn Spanish!

Most people are daunted by the idea of learning a language. They think it's impossible, even unfathomable. I remember as a junior in high school, watching footage of Jackie O giving a speech in French. I was so impressed and inspired by the ease at which she spoke this other language of which I could not understand one single word.

At that moment, I knew I had to learn at least one foreign language. I started with Spanish, later took on Mandarin, and most recently have started learning Portuguese. No matter how challenging and unattainable it may seem, millions of people have done it. You do NOT have to be a genius to learn another language. You DO have to be willing to take risks and make mistakes, sometimes even make a fool of yourself, be dedicated, and of course, practice, practice, practice!

This book will only provide you with the basics in order to get started learning the Spanish language. It is geared towards those who are planning to travel to a Spanish-speaking country and covers many common scenarios you may find yourself in so feel free to skip around to the topic that is most prudent to you at the moment. It is also focused on the Spanish of Latin America rather than Spain. Keep in mind, every Spanish-speaking country has some language details specific to them so it would be essential to do some research on the specific country or countries that you will visit.

I will now list some tips that I have found useful and should be very helpful to you in your journey of learning Spanish. I don't wish you luck because that will not get you anywhere- reading this book, dedicating yourself, and taking some risks will!

Important note

Due to the nature of this book (it contains charts, graphs, and so on), you will better your reading experience by setting your device on *LANDSCAPE* mode! (In case you're using an electronic device like Kindle).

Language Tips

Tip #1 - Keep an Open Mind

It may seem obvious but you must understand that languages are very different from each other. You cannot expect them to translate word for word. *'There is a black dog'* will not translate word for word with the same word order in Spanish. You have to get used to the idea of translating WHOLE ideas. So don't find yourself saying, *"Why is everything backwards in Spanish?"* because it may seem that way many times. Keep your mind open to the many differences that you will find in the language that go far beyond just the words.

Tip #2 - Take Risks

Be fearless. Talk to as many people as you can. The more practice you get the better and don't worry about looking like a fool when you say, *"I am pregnant"* rather than *"I am embarrassed,"* which as you will find out can be a common mistake. If anyone is laughing remember they are not laughing at you. Just laugh with them, move on, and LEARN from it, which brings us to our next tip.

Tip #3 - Learn from your Mistakes

It doesn't help to get down because you made one more mistake when trying to order at a restaurant, take a taxi, or just in a friendly conversation. Making mistakes is a HUGE part of learning a language. You have to put yourself out there as we said and be willing to make tons of mistakes! Why? Because what can you do with mistakes. You can LEARN from them. If you never make a mistake, you probably are not learning as much as you could. So every time you mess up when trying to communicate, learn from it, move on, and keep your head up!

Tip #4 - Immerse yourself in the language

If you're not yet able to go to a Spanish-speaking country, try to pretend that you are. Surround yourself with Spanish. Listen to music in Spanish, watch movies, TV shows, in Spanish. Play games on your phone, computer, etc. in Spanish. Another great idea is to actually put your phone, computer, tablet and/or other electronic devices in Spanish. It can be frustrating at first but in the end this exposure will definitely pay off.

Tip #5 - Start Thinking in Spanish

I remember being a senior in high school and working as a lifeguard at a fairly deserted pool. While I was sitting and staring at the empty waters, I would speak to myself or think to myself (to not seem so crazy) in Spanish. I would describe my surroundings, talk about what I had done and what I was going to do, etc.

While I was riding my bike, I would do the same thing. During any activity when you don't need to talk or think about anything else, keep your brain constantly going in Spanish to get even more practice in the language. So get ready to turn off the English and jumpstart your Spanish brain!

Tip #6 - Label your Surroundings/Use Flashcards

When I started to learn Portuguese, I bought an excellent book that included stickers so that you could label your surroundings. So I had stickers all over my parents' house from the kitchen to the bathroom that labeled the door, the dishes, furniture, parts of the house, etc. It was a great, constant reminder of how to say these objects in another language. You can just make your own labels and stick them all over the house and hope it doesn't bother your family or housemates too much!

Tip #7 - Use Context clues, visuals, gestures, expressions, etc.

If you don't understand a word that you have heard or read, look or listen to the surrounding words and the situation to help you. If you are in a restaurant and your friend says, "I am going to ??? a sandwich." You can take a guess that she said *order* or *eat* but you don't have to understand every word in order to understand the general meaning. When you are in a conversation use gestures, expressions, and things around you to help communicate your meaning. Teaching English as a second language to young learners taught me this. If you act everything out, you are more likely to get your point across. If you need to say the word *bird* and you don't know how you can start flapping your arms and chirping and then you will get your point across and possibly learn how to say *bird*. It may seem ridiculous but as I said, you have to be willing to look silly to learn another language and this greatly helps your language communication and learning.

Tip #8 - Circumlocution

Circumlo... what? This is just a fancy word for describing something when you don't know how to say it. If you are looking to buy an umbrella and don't know how to say it, what can you do? You can describe it using words you know. You can say, it is something used for the rain that opens and closes and then hopefully someone will understand you, help you, and maybe teach you how to say this word. Using circumlocution is excellent language practice and is much better than just giving up when you don't know how to say a word. So keep talking even if you have a limited vocabulary. Say what you can and describe or act out what you can't!

SECTION 1: THE BASICS

Chapter 1: Getting the Pronunciation Down

Below I will break down general Spanish pronunciation for the whole alphabet dividing it into vowels and consonants. One great thing about Spanish is that the letters almost always stay consistent as far as what sound they make. Unlike English in which the vowels can make up to 27 different sounds depending on how they are mixed. Be thankful that you don't have to learn English or at least have already learned English. There are of course some sounds in Spanish that we never make in English and you possibly have never made in your life. So get ready to start moving your mouth and tongue in a new way that may seem strange at first but as I keep saying, practice makes perfect!

The charts on the next page will explain how to say the letter, pronounce it, and if there is an example in an English word of how to say it I put it in the right column.

Vowel Sounds

Vowel	How to say the letter	How to pronounce it in a word	As in...
a	Ah	Ah	T<u>a</u>co
e	Eh	Eh	<u>E</u>gg
i	Ee	Ee	<u>E</u>asy
o	Oh	Oh	<u>O</u>pen
u	Oo	Oo	B<u>oo</u>k

Consonant Sounds

Consonant	How to say the letter	How to pronounce it in a word	As in...
b	b<u>eh</u>	similar to English b	
c	c<u>eh</u>	k after *a, o,* or *u* s after *e* or *i*	<u>c</u>at <u>c</u>ereal
ch	ch<u>eh</u>	ch	<u>ch</u>eese
d	d<u>eh</u>	a soft d (place your	<u>th</u>ree

		tongue at the back of your upper teeth)	
f	efe	F	free
g	geh	h before i or e g before a, o, u	him go
h	ache	silent	
j	hota	H	him
k	kah	K	karaoke
l	ele	like English l with tongue raised to roof of mouth	
ll	eye	Y	yes
m	eme	M	money
n	ene	N	no
ñ	enye	Ny	canyon
p	peh	like English p but you don't aspirate	

Consonants continued

Consonant	How to say the letter	How to pronounce it in a word	As in…
Q	koo	k (q is always followed by u like English)	quilt
R	ere	* at the beginning of a word you must roll your r's by vibrating tongue at roof of mouth * in the middle of a word it sounds like a soft d	
rr	erre	roll your r's as mentioned above	
S	ese	Like English s	sorry
T	teh	a soft English t, the tongue touches the back of the upper teeth	

V	veh	like Spanish b	boots

Consonants continued

Consonant	How to say the letter	How to pronounce it in a word	As in…
w	dobleveh	like English w	water
x	equis	*Between vowels and at the end of a word, it sounds like the English *ks*. *At the beginning of a word, it sounds like the letter *s*.	*box *sorry
y	igriega	like English y	yellow
z	seta	s	six

Note: If you're not sure how to pronounce a word, one thing you can do is type it in *Google translate* then click on the little speaker icon in the bottom left corner to hear the correct pronunciation.

To check out the rest of *"Learn Spanish In 7 DAYS! - The Ultimate Crash Course To Learning The Basics of The Spanish Language In No Time"*, **go to Amazon and look for it right now!**

Ps: You'll find many more books like these under my name, Dagny Taggart. Don't miss them! Here's a short list:

- Learn **Spanish** In 7 Days!
- Learn **French** In 7 Days!
- Learn **German** In 7 Days!
- Learn **Italian** In 7 Days!
- Learn **Portuguese** In 7 Days!

- Learn **Japanese** In 7 Days!
- Learn **Chinese** In 7 Days!

- Learn **Russian** In 7 Days!

- Learn Any Language FAST!

- How to Drop Everything & Travel Around The World

About the Author

Dagny Taggart is a language enthusiast and polyglot who travels the world, inevitably picking up more and more languages along the way.

Taggart's true passion became learning languages after she realized the incredible connections with people that it fostered. Now she just can't get enough of it. Although it's taken time, she has acquired vast knowledge on the best and fastest ways to learn languages. But the truth is, she is driven simply by her motive to build exceptional links and bonds with others.

She is inspired everyday by the individuals she meets across the globe. For her, there's simply not anything as rewarding as practicing languages with others because she gets to make friends with people from all that come from a variety of cultures. This, in turn, has broadened her mind and thinking more than she would have ever imagined it could.

Of course, as a result of her constant travels, Taggart has become an expert on planning trips and making the most of time spent out of what she calls her "base" town. She jokes that she's practically at the nomad status now, but she's more content to live that way.

She knows how to live on a manageable budget weather she's in Paris or Phnom Penh. She knows how to seek out the adventures and thrills, no doubt, lying in wait at any city she visits. She knows that reflection on each every experience is significant if she wants to grow as a traveler and student of the world's cultures.

Because of this, Taggart chooses to share her understanding of languages and travel so that others, too, can experience the same life-altering benefits she has.

Printed in Great Britain
by Amazon.co.uk, Ltd.,
Marston Gate.